NED, THE

Dan has a pet cat, Ned.

The cat has a big cod.

Get off the bed, bad cat!

Ned, get off the hat!

Ned is on the van!
Get off, Ned!

Ned has a nap...on Dan.

JUMPING JACK GAME

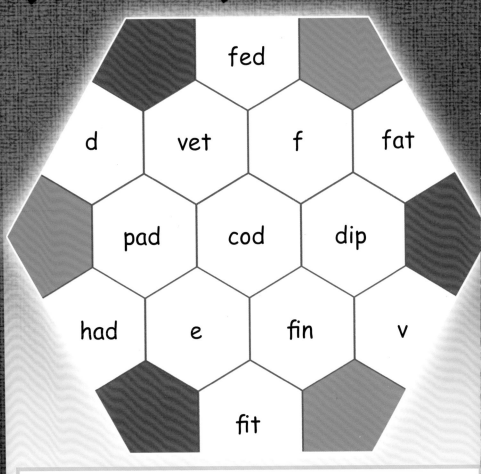

This is a game for two players. Each player has three counters, each set a different colour. Players choose to be Red or Blue and place one counter on each of their colours. Players take turns to move a counter by sliding it into an adjacent space or by jumping over their opponent's counter into an empty space. When a player lands on a word, he/she must read the word aloud. The winner is the first player to get all three of his/her counters in a straight line.